Nasir the Paleontologist

written by **Dwayna Williams**

illustrated by Kaviya Pugazhendi

Skylight Books

AN IMPRINT OF TANDEM LIGHT PRESS

Atlanta, GA

Tandem Light Press
950 Herrington Rd.
Suite C128
Lawrenceville, GA 30044

Copyright © 2024 by Dwayna Williams

Tandem Light Press paperback edition 2024

ISBN: 979-8-3302636-0-8
Library of Congress Control Number: 2024944385

PRINTED IN THE UNITED STATES OF AMERICA

ACKNOWLEDGMENTS

Without becoming a mother, I could never have imagined creating a children's book of this magnitude. Nasir has pushed me to expand my knowledge, and as a mompreneur, teaching him at home has been beyond beautiful. I'm thankful for my co-creator and son Nasir, who made me a mom and challenged me to learn about his interests. With my passion for diversity, dedication to representation, and Nasir's creativity, I'm honored to create this book for all parents and guardians, especially those of color. As a mom of two kings, I cherish offering them representation and fostering imagination.

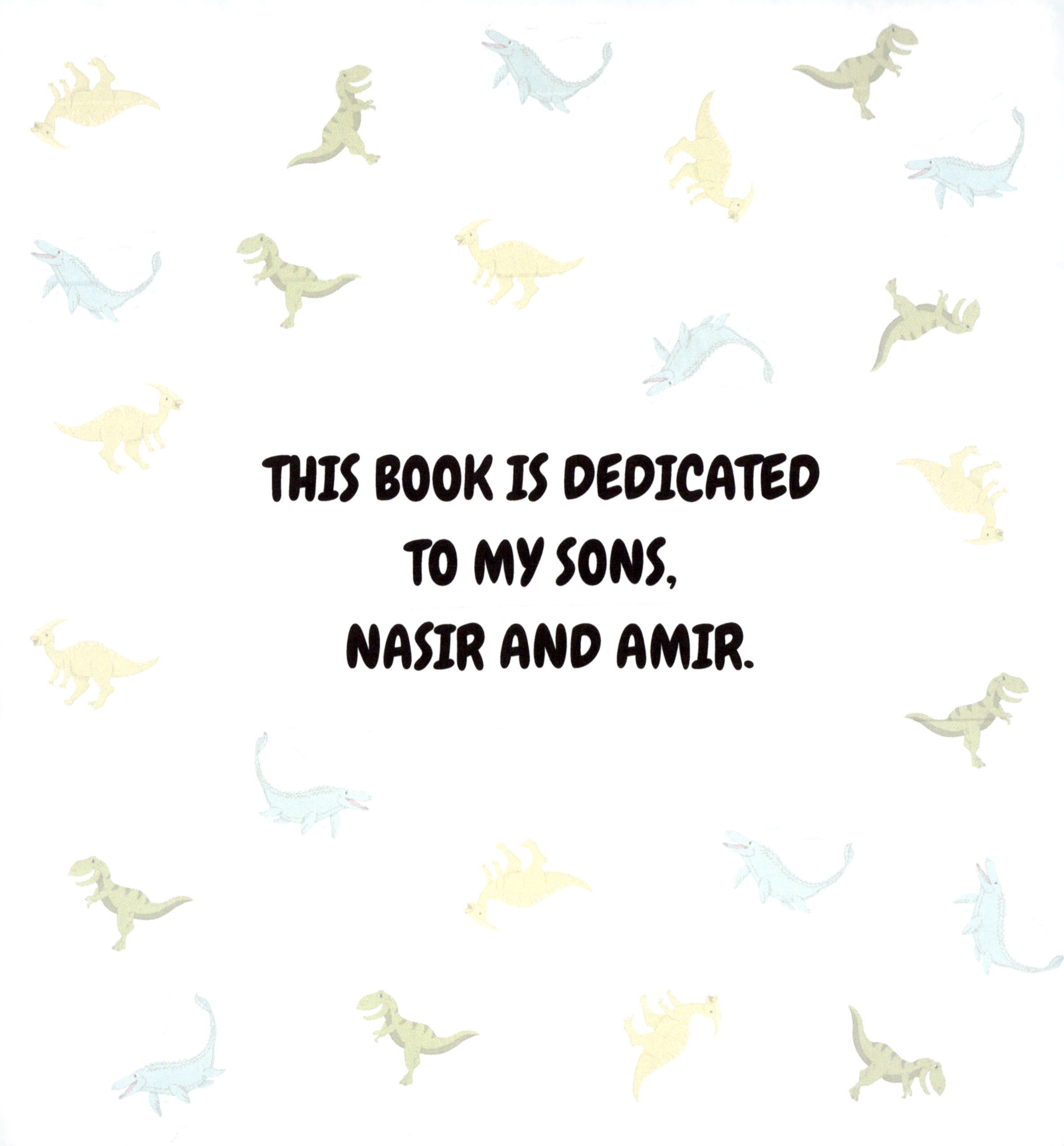

THIS BOOK IS DEDICATED
TO MY SONS,
NASIR AND AMIR.

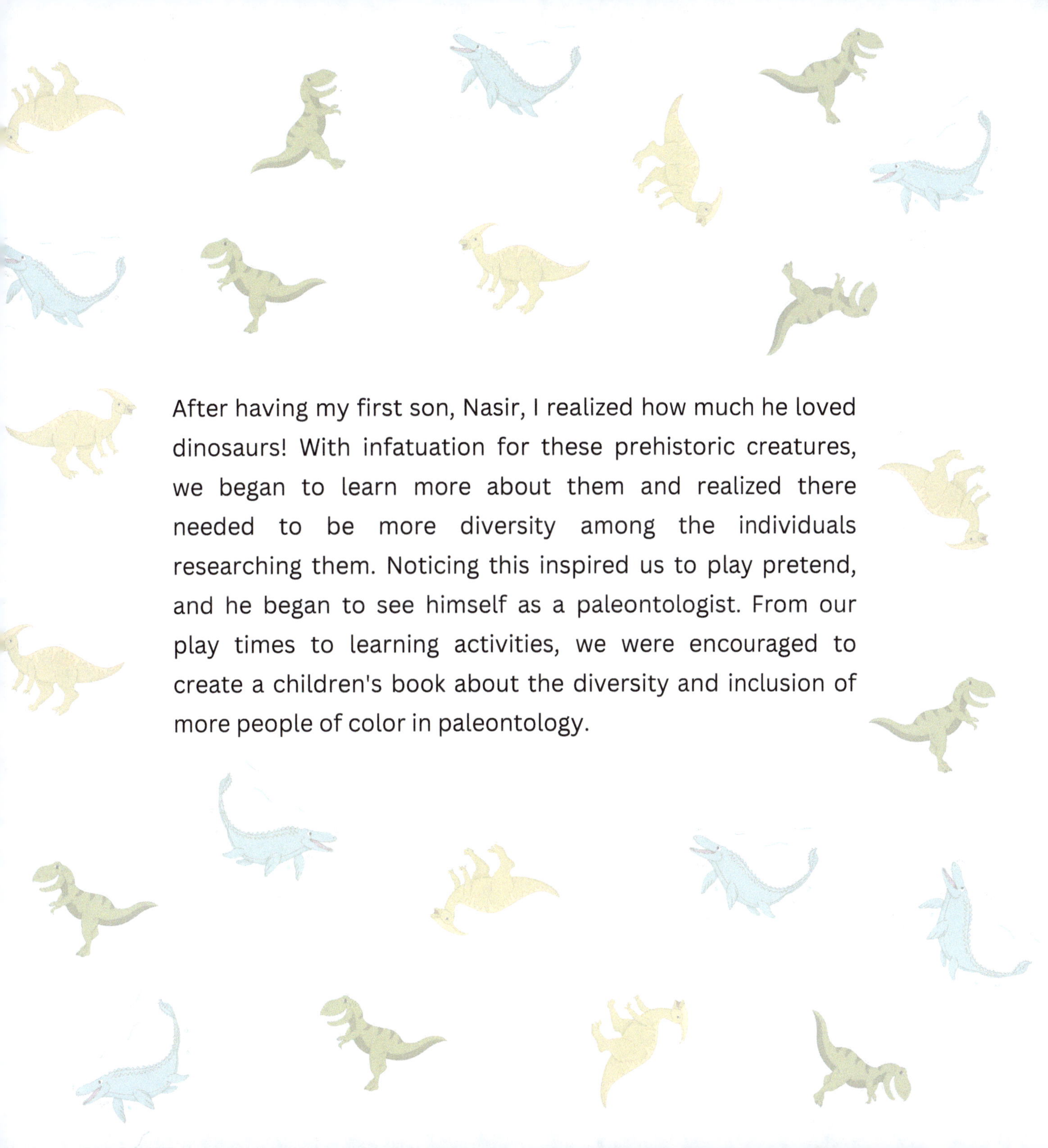

After having my first son, Nasir, I realized how much he loved dinosaurs! With infatuation for these prehistoric creatures, we began to learn more about them and realized there needed to be more diversity among the individuals researching them. Noticing this inspired us to play pretend, and he began to see himself as a paleontologist. From our play times to learning activities, we were encouraged to create a children's book about the diversity and inclusion of more people of color in paleontology.

Imagination can impact a **future**

that does not exist.

-Dwayna Williams

On a bright Saturday morning, Nasir woke up ready to take on a day of adventure.

After his
favorite meal
of the day,
breakfast,
RAWR

he got **dressed**
and **returned**
for **outside**
playtime.

"Hmmm. What should I play today?"

"I know! Today, I'm going on a hunt to find my favorite dinosaurs!"

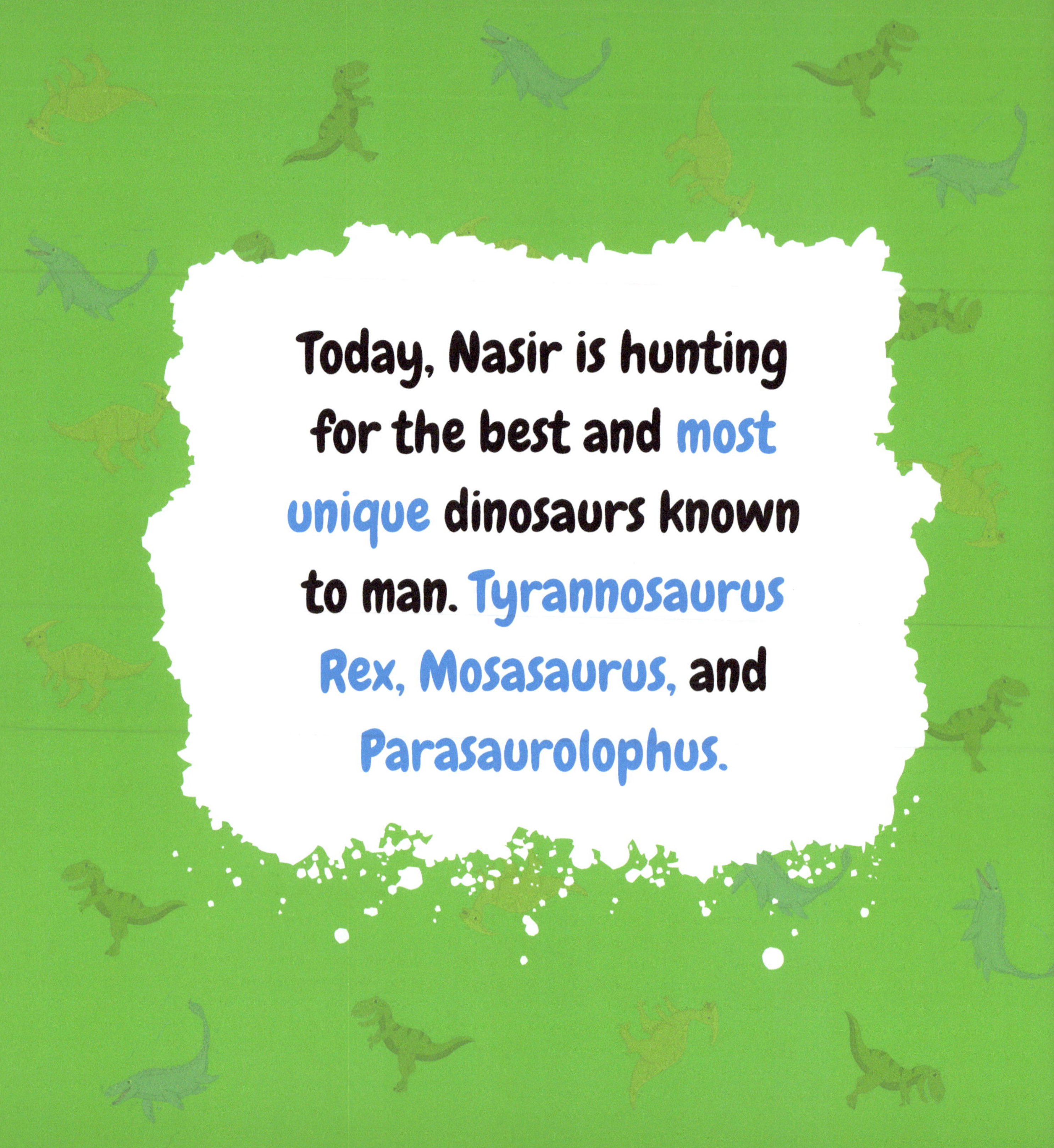

Today, Nasir is hunting for the best and most unique dinosaurs known to man. Tyrannosaurus Rex, Mosasaurus, and Parasaurolophus.

"Time for my paleontologist gear!"

"Will you help me find my favorite dinosaur friends?"

"Call me,
Nasir the
Paleontologist!"

"We're going on a hunt
for prehistoric dinosaurs.
On a hunt, we go!
We're looking for my
dino friends.
On a hunt, we go!"

Nasir sets off for his adventure.
LAND ROVER

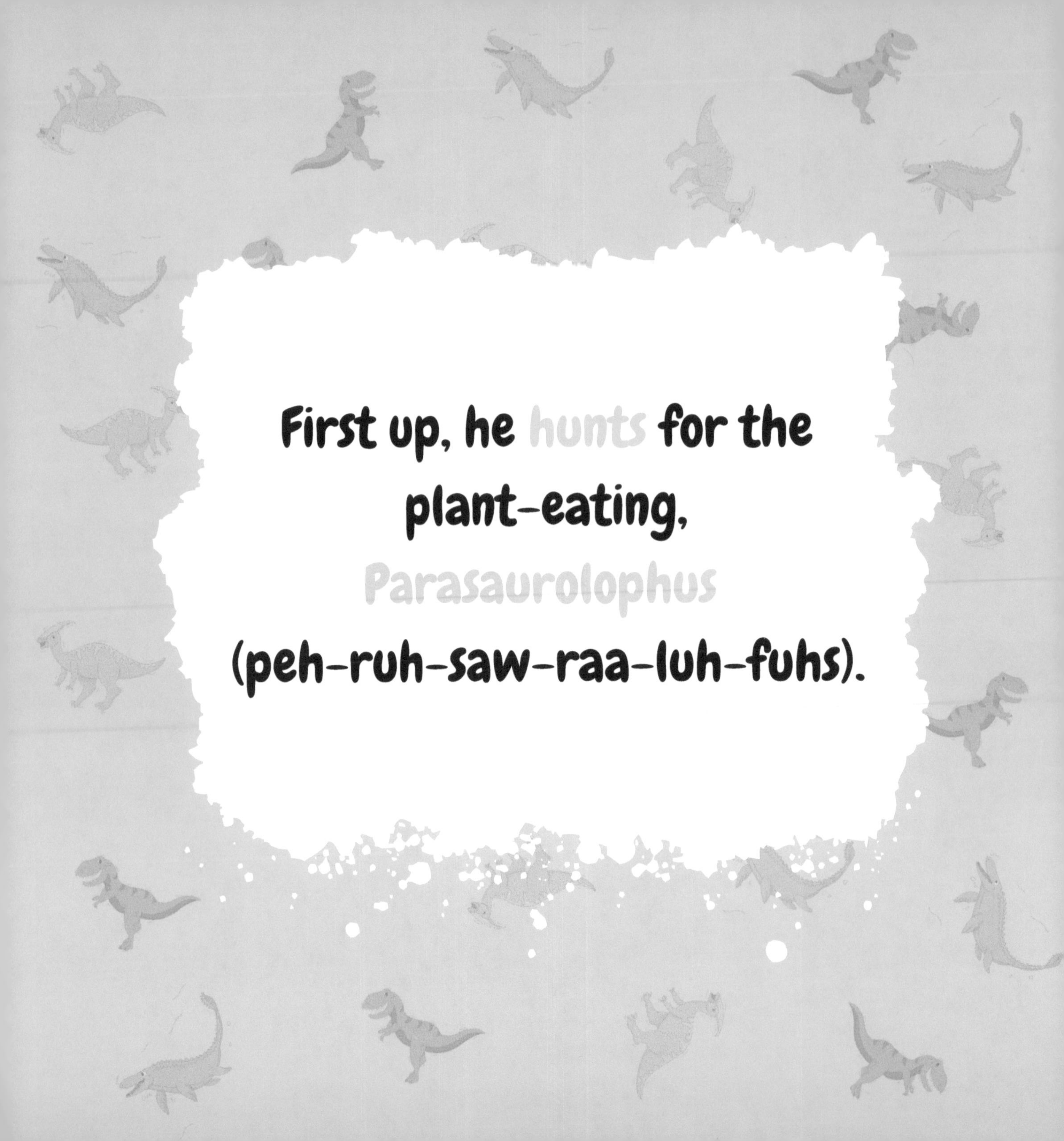

First up, he hunts for the
plant-eating,
Parasaurolophus
(peh-ruh-saw-raa-luh-fuhs).

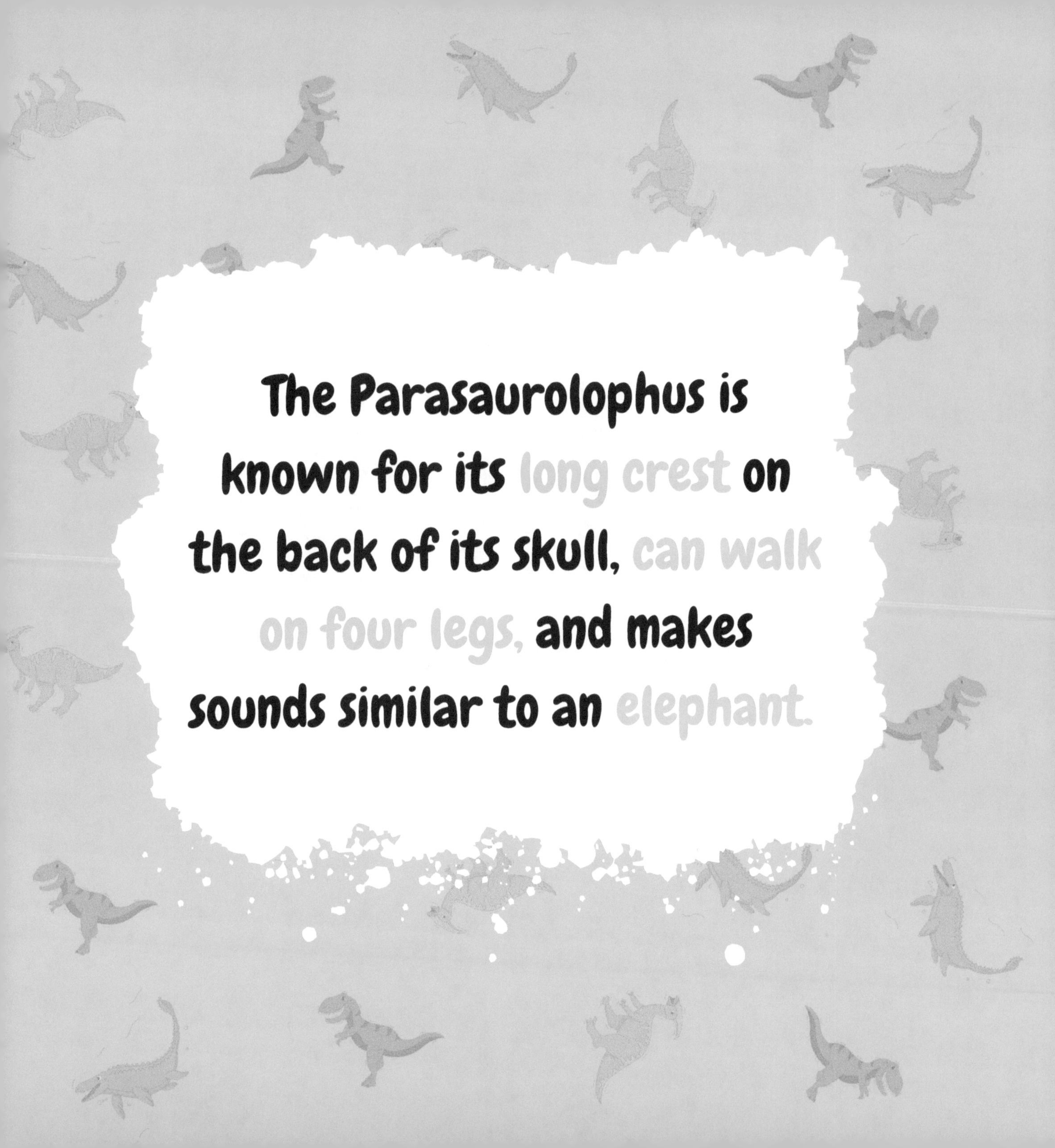

The Parasaurolophus is known for its long crest on the back of its skull, can walk on four legs, and makes sounds similar to an elephant.

"We can find my dino friend near the mountains and seashore!"

Nasir hears a sound.
It sounds like a Parasaurolophus.
Does it look like a Parasaurolophus?

"Yes, yes! It's him!" Nasir squeals.
He has a long crest on his skull, sounds like an elephant, walks on four legs, and eats grass.

"Hey my friend, hop in!"

Now, it's time to hunt for
the next dinosaur, Mosasaurus
(Moe-za-sore-us).

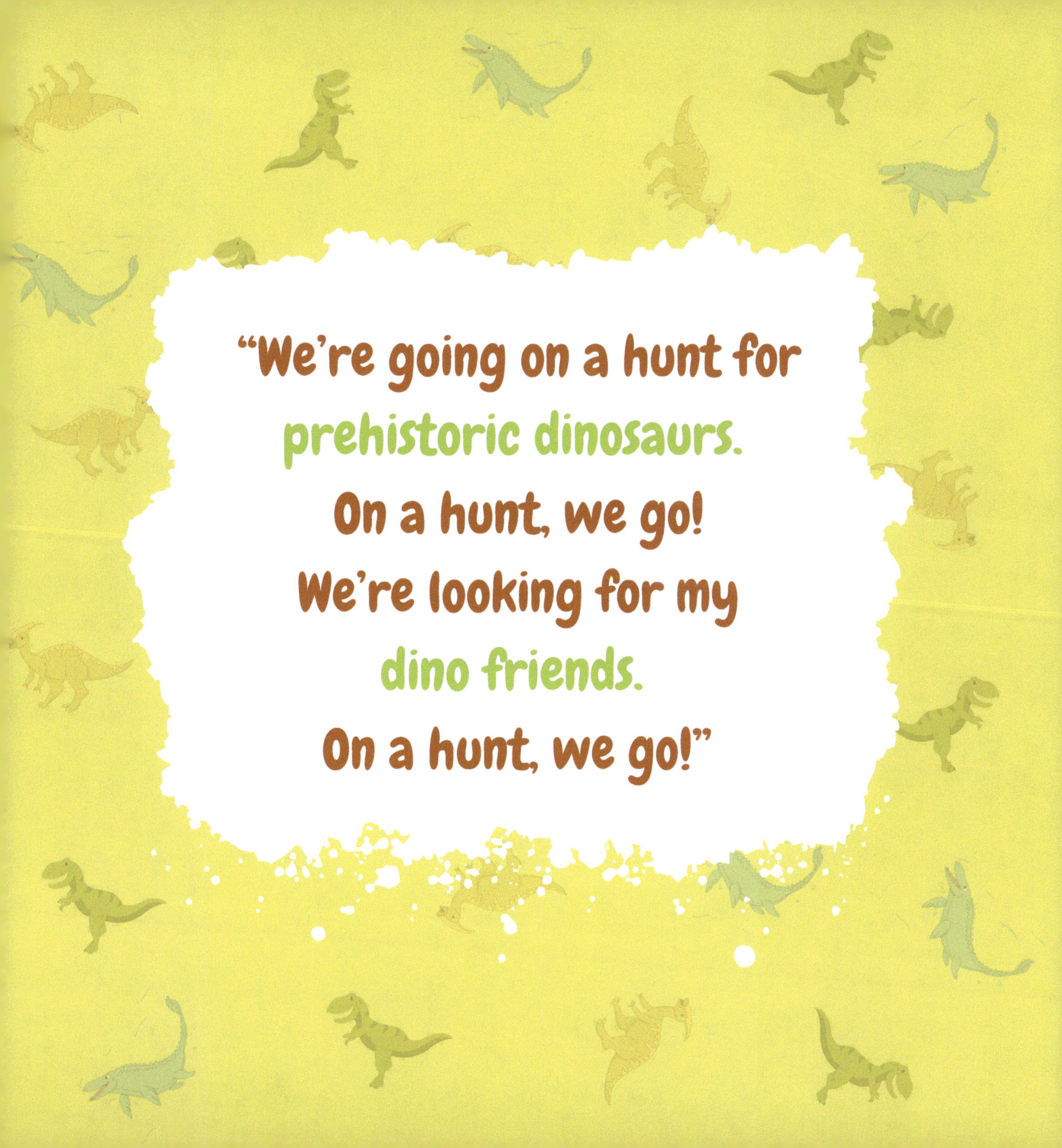
"We're going on a hunt for prehistoric dinosaurs.
On a hunt, we go!
We're looking for my dino friends.
On a hunt, we go!"

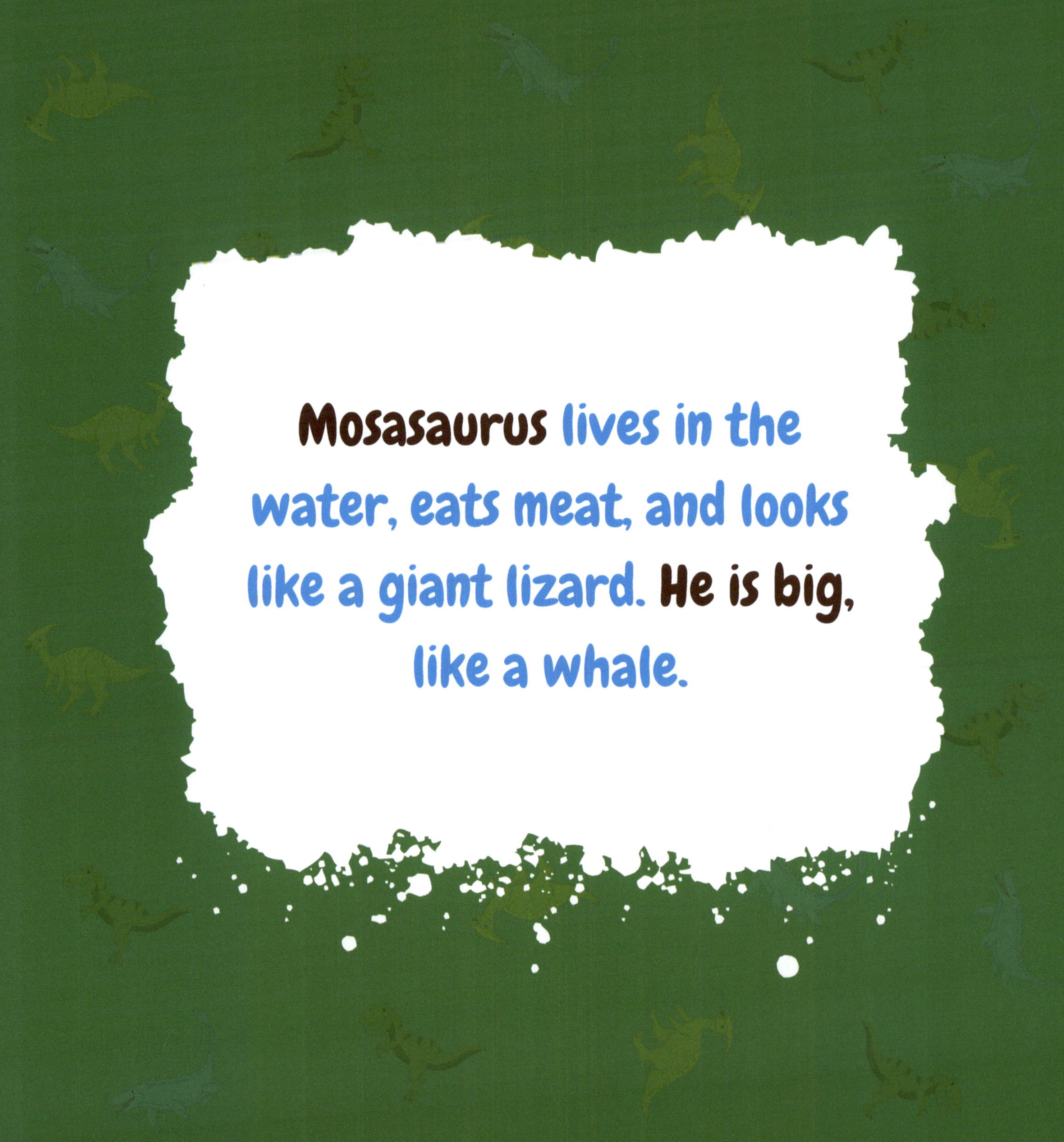

Mosasaurus lives in the water, eats meat, and looks like a giant lizard. He is big, like a whale.

"We can find Mosasaurus in the
Atlantic Ocean."

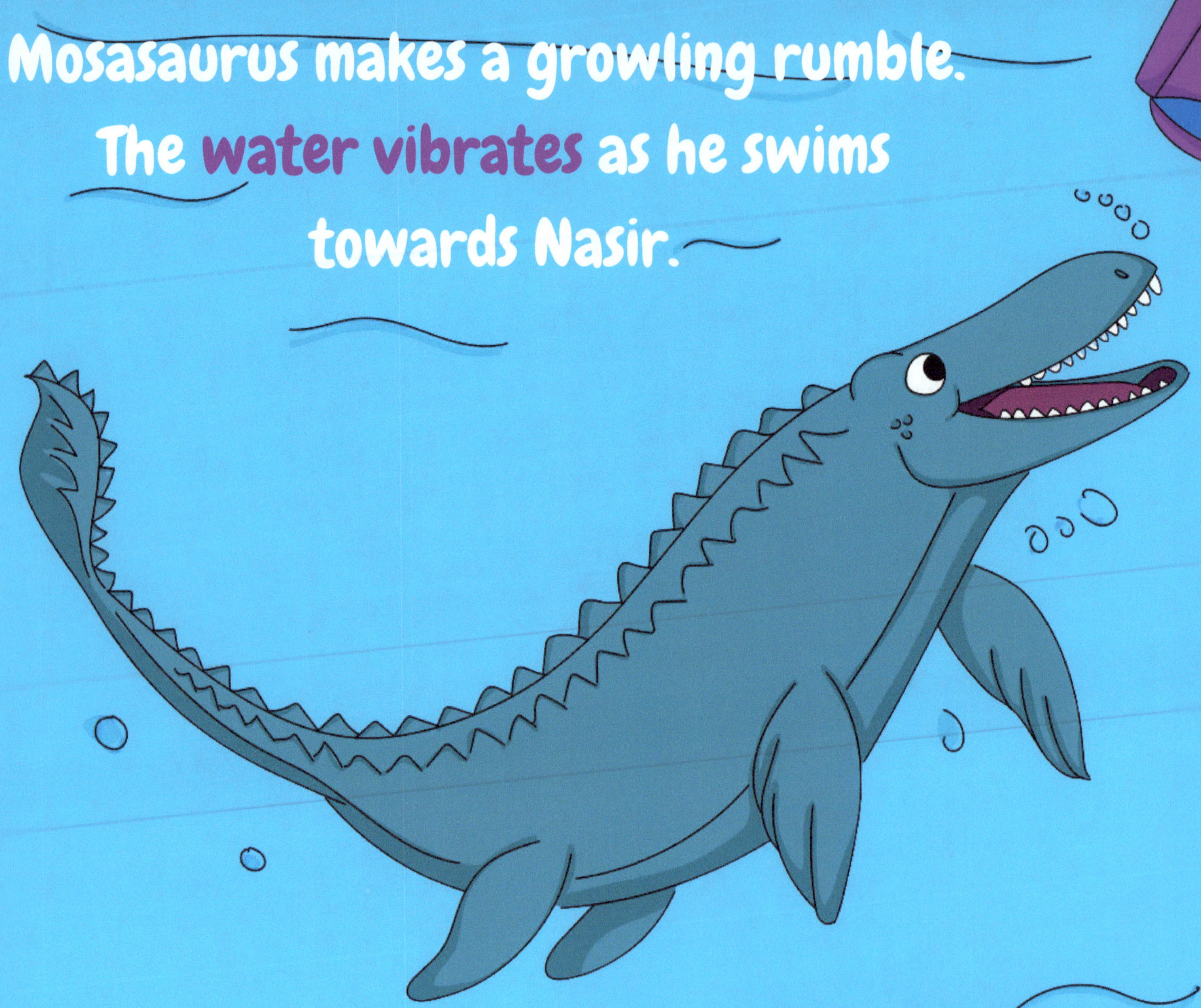

Mosasaurus makes a growling rumble.
The **water vibrates** as he swims
towards Nasir.

"Hey Mosasaurus, **it's playtime!**
Hop in the back and let's go!"

Last on the list is
Tyrannosaurus Rex
(tr·a·nuh·saw·ruhs reks),
T-Rex, for short.
He is Nasir's best friend.

"We're going on a hunt for prehistoric dinosaurs.

On a hunt, we go!

We're looking for my dino friends.

On a hunt, we go!"

T-Rex is a big-headed giant with strong jaws, teeth, a tail, and tiny arms.

He makes a powerful low rumble sound and hisses like a crocodile.

Nasir usually finds him in the forest near the rivers where Triceratops lives.

"Let's see if
we can locat
his footsteps!

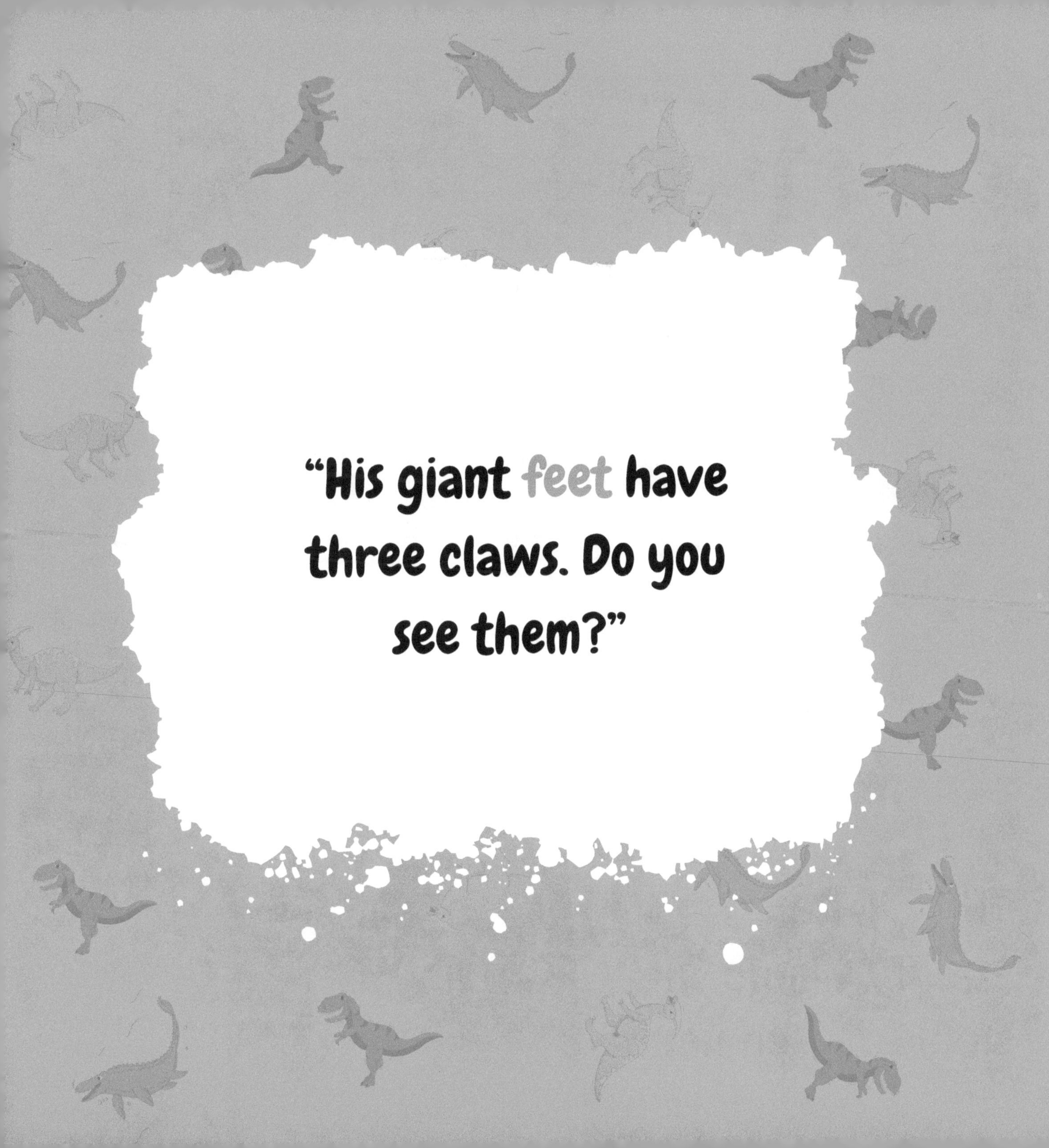

"His giant feet have three claws. Do you see them?"

"Nasir!"
T-Rex shouts.
"Hey, T-Rex! I knew I would find you! I missed you."

Nasir was excited he had all
his dino friends together
for playtime.

He had plans to play all day!

First, they played catch the bone. T-Rex won!

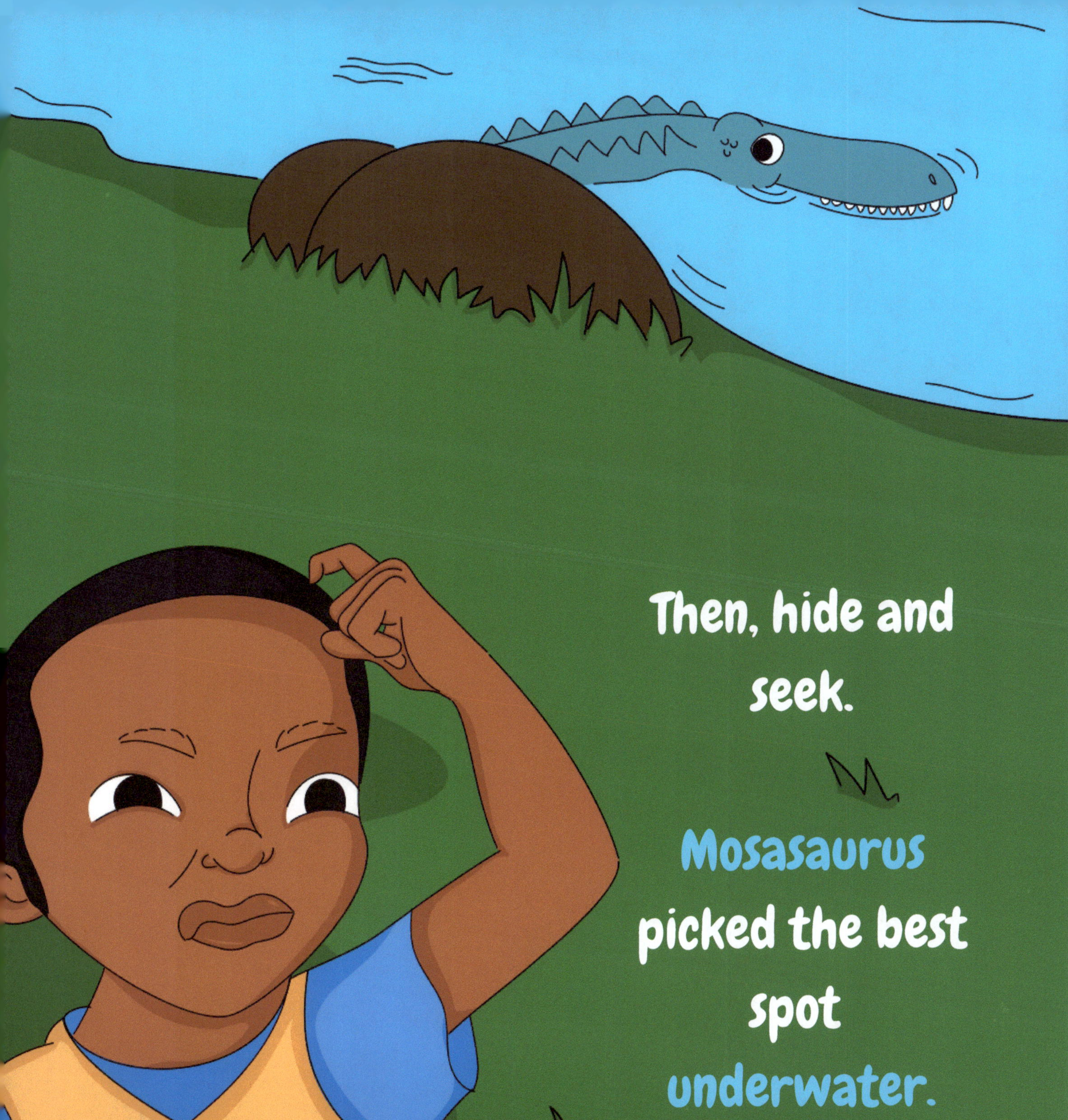
Then, hide and seek.

Mosasaurus picked the best spot underwater.

And next, they played tag.

Parasaurolophus won!
He had so much practice running
in herds with his family.

Nasir also taught them
his new Taekwondo moves.
They all had so much fun.

Nasir and T-Rex taught
their dino friends
a new dance.

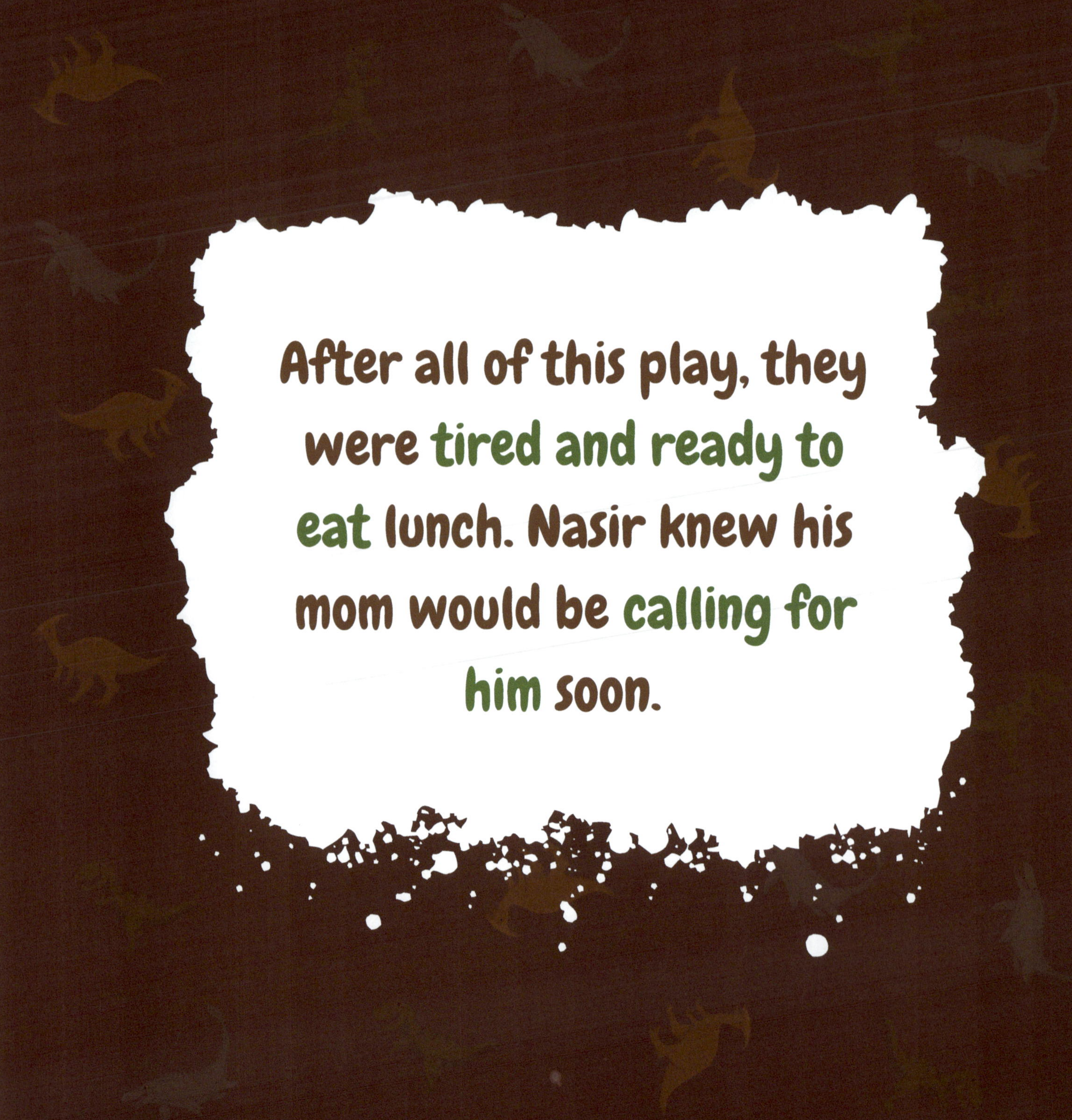

After all of this play, they were tired and ready to eat lunch. Nasir knew his mom would be calling for him soon.

Nasir takes everyone back home in his jeep, says his goodbyes, and then hears his mom shout, "Nasir! Come inside. It's time for lunch!"

Nasir's forest turns back into his backyard.
He walks toward the house with a huge grin on his face.

"Did you have as much fun as I did learning about my dino friends?"

"I really hope you can join me on my next adventure. See you next time!"

About the Author

Dwayna Williams is the co-founder of TGND Consulting. She describes herself as a "millennial mompreneur" and finds joy in empowering other millennial moms to pursue their dreams through entrepreneurship. Dwayna has extensive experience amplifying the public presence of change-makers, purpose-driven entrepreneurs, and subject matter experts and is constantly seeking new and innovative ways to promote buzz-worthy ideas. **Scan the QR code to follow adventures with Nasir:**

www.ingramcontent.com/pod-product-compliance
Lightning Source LLC
Chambersburg PA
CBHW042001110726

48006CB00004B/951